FRANKENSTEIN

by Mary Shelley

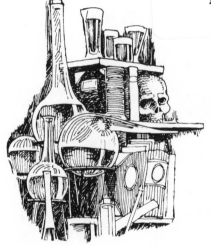

Abridged and adapted by T. Ernesto Bethancourt

Illustrated by James McConnell

A PACEMAKER CLASSIC

Fearon Education
a division of
David S. Lake Publishers
Belmont, California

Pacemaker Classics

The Adventures of Tom Sawyer
The Deerslayer
Dr. Jekyll and Mr. Hyde
Frankenstein
Great Expectations
Jane Eyre
The Jungle Book
The Last of the Mohicans
The Moonstone
Robinson Crusoe
A Tale of Two Cities
The Three Musketeers
The Time Machine
Treasure Island
20,000 Leagues Under the Sea
Two Years Before the Mast

Copyright © 1986 by David S. Lake Publishers, 500 Harbor
Boulevard, Belmont, California 94002. All rights reserved. No
part of this book may be reproduced by any means, transmitted,
or translated into a machine language without written permission
from the publisher.

Library of Congress Catalog Card Number: 84-62178

ISBN 0-8224-9257-1

Printed in the United States of America

1. 9 8 7 6 5 4 3

Contents

Introduction

Frankenstein is probably one of the best-known horror stories in the world. Many people have heard the story of the "mad doctor" who uses dead bodies to create a monster that turns bad and kills people.

Many movies have been made of the Frankenstein story. In most movies, the story has been changed. When you read the book, you may find some surprises. For example, "Frankenstein" is the name of the scientist—not the name of the monster. The monster has a personality that also might surprise you. And Frankenstein himself is not just a "mad scientist." He hopes to help people with his work.

Most people don't know that *Frankenstein* was written to win a bet. One evening in 1816, Mary Shelley, her husband, and a friend were sitting around the fire. They were telling ghost stories. They decided to see who would be the first to write a new kind of horror story. The other two people never finished their stories. But Mary Shelley began writing the next day. In a short time, she had written a horror story that would never be forgotten.

Opening Letters

To: Mrs. Saville, England
December 11, 17_ _

Dear Sister,

You'll be happy to know that, so far, nothing has gone wrong on this, my great adventure. And you had been so worried about me! I arrived yesterday. My first job is to let my sister know that I am all right.

I have high hopes for the trip ahead of me. I am already far north of London. As I walk the streets of this city, I feel a cold wind upon my cheeks. It makes me feel so happy. Can you understand this feeling? This wind is blowing from where I am going: the North Pole.

Although I try, I can't think of the Pole as a place with ice and snow all the time. Yes, I know that everyone thinks about it that way. But no one has ever set foot on the Pole. To me, it is a place of beauty and peaceful seas. The sun shines all the time. Who knows what wonders I will see there?

I have dreamed of this trip all my life. Do you remember Uncle Thomas's library? He had so many books about great sea trips to the Far North

Pacific. I read every one of them when I was a boy. I was going to be a great explorer. Then, when Father died, his will did not allow me to go.

But I always kept my dream. Uncle Thomas is gone now, and I have the money. I must go. I know that I was meant to do something really great with my life. I believe that this trip is that great thing. I have been getting ready for it. I have spent a lot of time in cold weather. That way, I'll be used to the weather near the North Pole. And I have sailed on boats that go as far north as fishing boats can go.

Now I must travel on land to Archangel. At this time of year, travel is easy. The horse-drawn sleds almost fly over the ice and snow. When I get to Archangel, I will rent a boat, and get some men to sail it. Then we will travel on to the North Pole.

Your loving brother,

R. Walton

To: Mrs. Saville, England
March 28, 17_ _

Dear Sister,

The time passes slowly here in Archangel. We are closed in by ice and snow. Yet I am happier than I have ever been in my life. I am beginning my great adventure. But something is missing. I have no friend to share it with. I want someone to talk to, someone to know my hopes and fears.

I have good sailors and a good captain. We are eager to leave. But we have to wait. The weather must clear up before we can sail. It was a terrible winter, but spring has come early. Soon we will leave for the Pole. I keep wondering if I will ever see you again. For now, please keep writing to me. I may be able to get a letter now and then. Your letters cheer me up so much. Remember me with love, if you never hear from me again.

Your loving brother,

R. Walton

To: Mrs. Saville, England
July 7, 17_ _

Dear Sister:

I am writing a few fast lines to say that I am safe. I'm well on my way. This letter will reach England on a ship headed home from Archangel. I don't know when or if I will ever see England again.

We are now very far north. Big sheets of ice float by us, but they don't seem to bother the men. When the wind blows from the south, the weather is quite nice. But it's not nearly as warm as in England at this time of year.

3

Nothing much has happened so far—nothing worth writing about. I am still excited about my adventure. I will succeed. I must succeed!

I must end this letter now. May heaven bless my dear sister!

Your brother,
R. Walton

To: Mrs. Saville, England
August 5, 17_ _

Dear Sister,

Something strange has happened. I must write it down. There is no one out here to take this letter to England. So you'll probably see me in person before this letter reaches you. Still, I must tell you what has happened.

Last Monday (July 31) we were in a dangerous spot. Ice and fog were all around us. We were afraid that we might run into floating ice. We stopped the ship for a while.

At about two o'clock in the afternoon, the fog cleared. When it did, all we could see for miles was solid ice. The men were worried and so was I. Then we saw the strangest thing.

We saw a dog sled out on the ice. It was about a half mile away. The figure in the dog sled looked like a man. But he was the size of a giant! We watched the sled until it was lost from sight. Where had this giant come from? We knew we were hundreds of miles from land.

A few hours later, the heavy ice that trapped our ship began to break up. But it was getting late in the day. We decided that we wouldn't start to move again until the next morning.

When I went out on deck the next morning, I saw some sailors leaning over the side of the ship. They seemed to be talking to someone on the ice below. I went over to the side and looked.

On a piece of floating ice I saw a dog sled. It was like the one we had seen the day before. But only one dog remained alive. There was a man in the sled. I would have thought he'd be an Eskimo, this far north. But this man was from Europe.

My captain was talking to the man on the ice. "Here is the master of this ship," he said. "He will not allow you to die in the sea."

I looked at the man. He looked very cold and tired. I told him that we would be happy to take him with us. The man gave me a strange answer. He said, "Before I come on board your ship, will you please tell me where you are going?"

I couldn't believe my ears! Here was this poor fellow, nearly dead from being out on the ice and snow. He was hundreds of miles from land. Yet before he'd let me save his life, he had to know

where we were headed! I explained that we were going to the North Pole. He seemed pleased, and agreed to come on board.

You should have seen the shape he was in. He was as thin as a rail. He looked as if he had been through a lot of trouble and pain. I had never seen a man in such bad shape.

We did what we could for him. We gave him a drink, and rubbed his arms and legs. After a while, he was able to eat some soup. Two days went by before the man was able to speak. He was a sad fellow, always looking out to sea. He spoke to no one.

The men were dying to know about him. What was he doing out here on the ice? What made him take such a chance with his life? But he was still very weak. I wouldn't allow the men to bother him with questions. Finally, my captain asked him why he had come so far on such a dangerous trip.

"I am after someone who ran away from me," he said.

"This man you are after, was he traveling the same way as you? On a dog sled?" asked the captain.

"Yes."

"Then I think we saw him," the captain said. "We saw a dog sled the day before we picked you up. A man was in it. He was riding across the ice."

Suddenly, the man was full of questions. Which way had the sled gone? How long ago? What did the other man look like? Later, when the man was alone with me, he said, "I know there are many things you would like to know about me. But you are too kind to ask."

"I felt it was none of my business," I answered. "Besides, you have been so sick. It wasn't the right time to ask."

The man asked me if I thought the breaking ice had destroyed the other dog sled. I told him I couldn't say for sure. The ice had broken up late that night. The other driver might have reached safety before the ice broke up.

After that, he was a different man. He kept staying out on deck, watching the ice. He seemed to be searching for that other dog sled. I told him that he was too weak to stand on deck so much. But he still wouldn't go below. Finally, I promised to put a man on deck to watch for him. I promised the fellow he would be called if anything was spotted. Someone has stood on deck watching, ever since that day.

The stranger's health is getting better each day. But he stays quiet, and to himself. I am the only one he will speak to. He is a gentle man, and quite interesting. I find I want to be with him. Maybe he can be the friend I wished for!

August 13, 17_ _

I like this stranger better every day. I admire him, but at the same time I feel sorry for him. He looks very unhappy. Yet, he never talks about any sadness. My heart goes out to him. He is so gentle and so wise. He speaks beautifully, and I love to listen to him.

A few days ago, I told this man about my trip to the Pole. He listened very closely. I must have gotten carried away talking about my adventure. In no time, I told him about my life's dream. I told him how important this trip was to me. I told him that I had to go on, even if it cost my life, and the lives of some of my men. I said to him, "What is the life of a few men, when so much can be gained by science?"

As I said this, an awful look of sadness came over his face. He covered his face with his hands. He let out a terrible cry. I didn't say anything. Then, at last, he spoke.

"Oh, you poor man!" he cried. "Do you share the same madness I have? Are you so far gone that you don't care about human life anymore? If you knew my story, you'd never feel the same way again."

Then he was quiet again. After a time, he spoke. He asked me about myself. He wanted to know about my childhood and my dreams. It didn't take long for me to tell him. I also talked about how lonely I had been and how much I wanted a friend.

9

"I agree with you," he told me. "Friends can be so important. Sometimes, it seems as if we are only half-made people. Our friends become that other part, and make us whole. I once had a friend like that. He was the finest person I ever knew. Now, he is gone. He is lost to me forever. I have lost everything. I think I will never again have a friend. I am doomed to be alone."

He fell silent then. I looked at this fine man, and had to wonder. Why was he so unhappy? How had he lost his dearest friend in the world? He must have read my mind. In a few moments he said to me, "I thank you for caring about me. But it's too late. There is only one reason for my life now. There is one thing I must do. After that, my life will be ended. I see in your face that you wish to help me. But I am beyond any help. And once you hear my story, you will know I am right."

Tomorrow, he will tell me his story. I plan to write it down in his own words as much as possible.

Your brother,
R. Walton

Chapter 1

My name is Victor Frankenstein. I grew up in Geneva, Switzerland. My family is one of the best-known families in Switzerland. For many years, members of my family held public office. My father was famous for his public service.

Perhaps I should tell you about how my father and mother met. One of my father's friends was a rich businessman. Once, a deal this man worked on went bad. But he kept his word to all the people who trusted him. He paid off everyone who had lost money. But he was left without a cent. He and his daughter became very poor. They had to move away from the city of Geneva.

My father heard that his friend had fallen on hard times. He went to visit him. When he saw the way his friend and his daughter were living, my father's heart almost broke. He offered help. But his friend was very proud. He refused any help. He was ill. The only money he had came from small jobs his daughter did for the people in town. When she wasn't working, the young woman spent most of her time taking care of her sick father.

My father heard that his friend was dying. My father, again, wanted to help. He went to visit his friend. He found the girl crying over her dead father's body. My father didn't want to see his old friend's daughter left out on the street. He took care of her. Two years later, they were married.

After the wedding, my father and mother traveled to many countries. Perhaps it was the years of being poor that did it, but my mother's health was not good. For this reason, they spent a lot of time in the warm weather of Italy. I was born in Italy on one of their vacations.

For years, I was their only child. I remember that those years were very happy. My father and mother loved each other very much. But there was enough love for me, their only son.

When I was five years old, my parents took another vacation to Italy. Because my mother was always interested in helping the poor, they visited a little hut on the shore of a lake. There, they found a poor farmer and his wife. The family had no money and very little food for their five children.

One of the children, a little girl, caught my mother's eye. This girl wasn't like the other children. She seemed different in little ways. There was a sweetness to the child that drew my mother to her. She asked the farmer about this little girl.

The little girl's name was Elizabeth. She was not the farmer's daughter. Her real father had been forced to leave Italy for a while. He had asked the farmer to take care of his little girl. When Elizabeth's father died in another country, she had no place to go. She stayed with the farmer and his family.

But then hard times came to this farmer. He had very little money. And besides Elizabeth, he had four children of his own. Life was hard for the family.

My mother had always wanted a little girl. She asked the farmer if she and my father could adopt Elizabeth. The farmer and his wife loved the little girl. But they knew that she would live a much happier life with my family. So they let my parents take Elizabeth.

I knew nothing of this. I was too young for my parents to talk about it to me. All my mother did was tell me, "I have a pretty present for my Victor. He shall have it tomorrow." The next day, she presented Elizabeth to me.

Elizabeth and I grew up together. There was only a year's difference in our ages. We never fought. We loved each other in a way brother and sister cannot. No tears, no ugly words ever darkened our days. We called each other "cousin" and shared a deep love until the day she died.

Elizabeth loved Switzerland. She loved the mountains and the lakes. She was always interested in art and beauty. I was different. While Elizabeth would get excited about how beautiful things were, I always wanted to know what made them the way they were. Even as a child, I was becoming a man of science.

When I was seven years old, my brother Ernest was born. At that time, my parents stopped traveling to different countries. We had a house in the city of Geneva. We also had a place in the country, on the shore of a lake. We spent most of our time at the country house. It was there, four years later, that my brother William was born.

Our family did not know a lot of people. I had only one close friend. His name was Henry, and he was the son of a Geneva businessman. Henry and I became best friends. He used to dream of the days of King Arthur. He always was making up plays about knights and fair ladies. He always wanted Elizabeth and me to act out these plays.

Henry, Elizabeth, and I spent our childhoods together. We were like three parts of one person. Elizabeth was the soul, Henry was the heart, and I was the mind. Henry kept telling stories of heroes and great adventurers. Elizabeth had her art. And I began to study science.

You must understand that I was quite young. I knew little about science. I read any books that I thought might explain the wonders of science. I found a number of these books in my father's library. They were by men who lived a long time ago. One day, my father found me reading one of these books.

"Ah, you're reading this?" my father said. "My dear Victor, don't waste your time on this. It is sad garbage."

If my father had explained to me that no one believed in these books anymore, it would have been different. Most of the stuff in the books was little more than "black magic." Science had already shown that these writers were silly. But I didn't know this. I was angry. My father thought that the books I liked were garbage! Instead of stopping reading these books, I found more like them.

Looking back on it, I guess I was foolish. I tried spells to change lead into gold. I tried to make devils appear. Of course, none of these spells worked. I might have gone on this way for years, but then something happened.

One night when I was fifteen years old, we were at our country house. A terrible storm came up. As I watched from my window, I saw lightning hit an oak tree. When the storm was over, I went out and looked at what was left of the tree. I thought that I would just find a burned tree. But the tree had been turned into small pieces of wood by the lightning. I was surprised. Why did this happen?

A friend of my father's was visiting us that day.

He was a scientist. He explained how lightning had destroyed the tree. Before this day, I didn't know much about electricity.

This was the true beginning of my life as a scientist. I forgot all about those silly books that were filled with magic spells. I began to study nature and to read books about true science. I felt as if the lightning had been a sign from heaven. It had pointed the way my life would go.

What I didn't know was that this sign could not have been from heaven. I didn't know that my study of science would someday destroy my life and all that I loved.

Chapter 2

When I was seventeen years old, my parents decided that I should go away to a university in Germany. I was ready to leave when Elizabeth got sick. It was scarlet fever. My mother took care of her. Elizabeth got better, but my mother caught scarlet fever.

She knew she was dying. She called Elizabeth and me to her bedside. "I have always wanted you two children to marry one day," she told us. "Now that day is close. I am so sad that I must leave you. But I hope we will meet again in another world."

She died quietly. We were all very sad. It didn't seem right for me to go off to the university right away. I stayed at home for a few more weeks. I spent most days with Elizabeth.

Finally, the time came for me to leave. My friend Henry came over that last day. I knew that everything in my life was about to change. Maybe that's why Elizabeth, Henry, and I spent this last day together. We had never been closer, or loved each other more. Little did I know that we would never share such happiness again. The next morning, I left for the university.

17

After a long hard trip, I arrived in Germany. The next day, I went to the university and met my teachers. The first one I saw was Dr. Krempe. He taught science. He knew a lot about science, but he was a rude man.

He asked me what science books I had read. I told him about the books with magic spells. He laughed out loud. "What a waste of time!" he said. "Nobody bothers with those books anymore. You'll have to start your studies all over again."

He gave me a list of books to buy. He told me about another teacher, Dr. Waldman. Dr. Waldman taught chemistry. I took Dr. Krempe's book lists. But I wasn't planning to go to his classes. His rude ways put me off too much.

About a week later, I stopped by the lecture hall to see what Dr. Waldman looked like. I was happily surprised. Waldman was everything Krempe was not. He spoke well, with a very pleasant voice. Where Krempe was hard, Waldman was smooth. And that man could teach! He started off with a history of chemistry:

"The old masters promised things they couldn't do: turn lead into gold, stay young forever. These were all empty dreams. But scientists of today are different. They don't promise much, but look at what they have done! We now know how blood moves through our bodies. We know what makes up the air we breathe. We are aiming at the skies, and we get closer every day. Who knows what wonders may come next?"

How Waldman's words excited me! I could hardly sleep that night. I went to see him the next morning. I told him the same things I had told Krempe. But Waldman didn't laugh at the books I had read. He said, "We owe a lot to those old writers. True, they were wrong. But don't you see? They started it all. Without them, science wouldn't be what it is today."

Waldman told me that he was happy that I wanted to study chemistry with him. "However, you should study *all* kinds of science—not just chemistry," he said. "Studying just one kind of science is like studying only one side of a building. All you know is that one side."

He took me to his workshop. He showed me how his machines worked. Then he gave me a long list of books to read. When I left Dr. Waldman's house, my life was changed.

I spent the next two years studying science. I didn't even go home for a visit. I lived for my books and classes. I made some discoveries in chemistry that made me well known at the university. Finally, the time had come to begin work on my own. But what would that work be?

I thought of going home to Geneva. I wanted to visit my family and friends. But then something happened that made me stay where I was.

Chapter 3

The wonder of life had always interested me. Not just in humans, but in animals as well. Just where did life come from? No one has ever known. Most of my studies had been in chemistry. Now I decided to study human biology.

To study life is also to study death. I wanted to see how death changed bodies. I cut into dead animals and people. I saw how death gives way to life. A human or animal dies, and its body gives food and life to worms. I know that cutting up dead bodies sounds horrible, but it didn't seem that way to me.

Then, like a flash of light, it came to me. It was so simple. Why hadn't anyone seen it before? I knew that I had come upon the secret of life! I knew that I could make things come to life!

I can see from your face that you would like to know this secret, too. But that cannot be. I cannot tell. If you hear my story to its end, you will see why. I tell you this: be happy that you do not know this secret. It's much better not to know.

When I found I could really create life, I had to stop to think. Should I start with simple animals? And if so, what ones? At first, I didn't think that I should try to make an animal like myself: a man. It would be too hard.

But then I thought about how things were changing in science all the time. New discoveries were being made every day. I was sure that if I had problems, I would find answers. I had to succeed. I

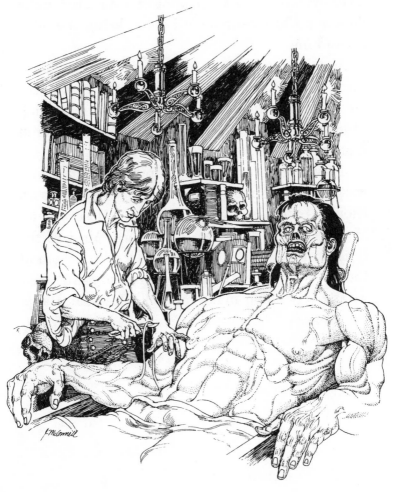

knew I would. For a month, I gathered my things together. Then I began.

What was I thinking at this time, you may ask? Was I like a man who had lost his mind? No, my friend, far from it. I was going to create a new kind of man. This man would love me more than a son loves his father. I also thought that if I could make lifeless parts live, maybe I could bring the dead back to life.

These thoughts kept me going. I shake when I think of the things I did. I robbed graves and cut up the dead bodies. I can still see all those staring, dead eyes. I stole bones and organs. The horror of it stays with me, even today.

My work became everything to me. I didn't write to my family, and I never went out with friends. I ate very little and began to lose weight. My eyes grew deep set in my face. Most of the time, I didn't wash. I worked in a secret room at the top of my house near the university. At times, what I was doing made me sick. But still, I kept working.

Chapter 4

Over a year passed. I received letters from my father. He was worried about me. But I couldn't stop. I couldn't write back. I had to finish my great project.

Then, one dark night in November, I came to the end of all my work. It was one o'clock in the morning. The rain fell against the window. My candle was nearly burned out. I put together all my instruments, so I could give life to the thing on my table. Then I saw the creature's yellow eyes open. It breathed hard, and its arms and legs shook.

How can I describe this thing I had worked so hard to make? He was very tall. I had chosen his face as beautiful. Beautiful? How wrong could I have been? His long hair was black and shiny. His teeth were white and perfect. But these things made the rest of him seem even more horrible. His yellow skin barely covered what was underneath it. His yellow eyes almost matched the color of his skin. He had straight black lips.

This was what I had worked on for almost two years. For this, I had gone without sleep and almost destroyed my health. I had worked for a beautiful dream of creating life. But in that moment, all beauty was gone. I was filled with horror. I ran from the workshop to my bedroom.

I kept walking around in the room. I couldn't sleep. I don't know how long I walked. Finally, I wore myself out. I fell down on the bed and went to sleep.

I dreamed I saw Elizabeth. She was young, healthy, and beautiful. But when I took her in my arms to kiss her, she changed. Her face looked dead. Then, for a moment, I thought I held the dead body of my mother in my arms. I could see worms crawling all over her dress.

I woke up with a start. The dim, yellow light of the moon came through my bedroom window. Then I saw IT—the thing I had created. He lifted my bedcovers. His yellow eyes looked straight at me. His black lips were set in a horrible grin. From his mouth came an awful sound. He may have been trying to talk. I don't know.

He reached toward me. Maybe he wanted to stop me from running. But I got around him and ran from the room. I ran outside. I spent the rest of the night in the yard, walking back and forth. When morning came, I began walking through town. I had no idea where I was going. I knew I couldn't go back to my house, where the creature waited.

After a time, I found myself at the place where stage coaches stopped. One was coming, and I saw

that it was from Geneva. As I watched it, the coach stopped. The door opened, and my friend Henry stepped out. He saw me right away.

"My dear Frankenstein," he said. "How glad I am to see you! And what luck that you are here to meet me!"

We shook hands warmly, and began to walk toward the university. When I saw Henry, I forgot the monster. I felt happy for the first time in months. It was almost as good as being back home. I thought of my father, my brothers, and dear Elizabeth. But what was Henry doing here? I asked him.

"You don't know how hard it was," Henry said. "I finally talked my father into letting me go to the university here. He will pay all my costs. We'll be schoolmates, Victor!"

He looked at me warmly. Then his face changed. "But how sick you look, Victor," he said. "I was going to yell at you for not writing. Your father and Elizabeth are worried about you. But you look as if you haven't slept in days."

"You're right, Henry," I said. "But it isn't sickness. I have been working very hard. I haven't been taking care of myself. But now, that work is over."

Of course, I didn't dare talk about my work. I didn't want anyone to know about it. Suddenly I saw where we had walked. We were in front of my house. What if that thing were still there, waiting? I had Henry wait outside, while I looked through the house. The monster wasn't there. Filled with joy, I went and brought Henry inside.

We were having breakfast when it happened. My joy turned into something else. I couldn't stop laughing. I began jumping around the room, still laughing.

"Victor, why are you acting this way?" Henry asked. "What's wrong?"

I began to cry. "Don't ask me!" I yelled. I threw my hands in front of my eyes. I thought I saw the monster come into the room. "He can tell you," I said. Suddenly, I felt as if the creature had grabbed me. "Oh, save me! Save me!" I cried. Then I fell to the floor in a fit. It was the beginning of a sickness that lasted for months.

Henry took care of me during that time. I didn't know who or where I was. Little by little, I began to come out of it. I began to see things around me and to talk with Henry. I was far from well, but I was coming back to the real world.

When I was better, Henry told me that classes were about to begin at the university. I knew that I didn't want to study science again. Every time I thought about science, I remembered the monster I had made. So, for the next six months, I went to Henry's classes with him. We studied history and languages.

Then the school year ended. I looked forward to leaving Germany. I wanted to go home and see my family again. It had been almost six years since I had been home.

I began to get ready to go back to Geneva. I expected a happy homecoming. But that was not to be.

Chapter 5

Just as I was about to leave for home, I received a letter from my father. Something terrible had happened. My youngest brother William was dead. He had been murdered!

The letter explained that the family had been walking together near Lake Geneva. William had gotten lost. They found him in the woods. My father wrote that William had "the print of the murderer's finger on his neck."

I went back to Switzerland right away. I had been so excited about this trip. Now this awful thing had happened. But the worst was yet to come.

When I got to Geneva, it was quite late. The city gates were shut. I spent the night in a nearby town. In the morning, I rented a small boat. My father's house was across the lake.

As I rowed, I saw a storm over a nearby mountain. The lightning flashed. The thunder roared. "Poor William," I thought. "Is this your funeral song?" I landed the boat, and began to walk toward my father's house. Lightning flashed again. For a moment, I thought I saw the shape of a person near some trees. This was near the spot where William's body had been found. Could the killer have returned?

Lightning flashed again, and my blood ran cold. There, in the flash of light, I saw it—the awful thing I had given life to. There could be no mistake about it. I saw that giant body and that horrible face. Then, in a second, he was gone. I tried to follow, but the monster was too fast. A minute later, the lightning flashed again. I saw the creature climbing the mountain. It was nearly

straight up and down, but he rose up the cliff like a fly.

I knew right away what had happened. The monster had killed my baby brother. Only something that wasn't human could have hurt such a sweet child as William. And what could I do about it? Who could catch such a strong creature? He could throw grown men around like babies. And I couldn't tell the truth to the police in Geneva. They would call me a madman and lock me up. No one would believe that a creature I had made from lifeless parts had killed my youngest brother!

When I got to my father's house, I found him almost mad with sorrow. My other brother Ernest was with him. Elizabeth had stayed in bed, crying. Somehow, she felt that she had caused William's death. She felt that if she hadn't let him wander off, William might still be alive.

Ernest began telling me about the murder. I wasn't listening to what he was saying. I had seen the monster, and this was very much on my mind. Then I heard Ernest say, "But since the murderer has been found . . . " Suddenly, I was all ears.

"The murderer has been found?" I asked. "How can that be? Who could be strong enough to follow him? I saw him, too, last night."

"I don't know what you mean," Ernest said to me. "Justine is the one being held." Justine was a young woman who had been adopted by our family many years before. I knew she loved William as much as we did. She had always been there to play with him and to take care of him.

"But that can't be," I said. "Justine would never harm little William."

"None of us thought so, either," Ernest replied. "But the police found something. You remember the little picture of mother? The one Father had made into a pin?"

"Yes, I do," I answered.

"Well, William wore that pin. He begged Father to let him wear it. Even though it was worth a lot of money, Father let him keep it. The pin was found in Justine's pocket."

"A mistake has been made," I said.

Yes, a mistake had been made. But I was the only one who knew it. Elizabeth didn't know what I knew. But she didn't believe that Justine would kill William. Elizabeth and I tried to help Justine. But we couldn't. There was a trial. Poor Justine was found guilty. She was hanged a few days later.

Can you know what went through my mind? I knew that the monster had killed William. But I couldn't tell anyone. No one would believe me. And all this trouble had come about because of me. I had created the monster. And because of my creation, both my brother William and dear Justine were dead!

Chapter

I felt that I was in a living hell during those months after William and Justine died. I knew that I had caused their deaths, and I felt that I was evil. I started spending more and more time alone. I could not face my loving family.

I began to take long walks. One day, I decided to climb a high mountain near my home. It was a steep climb, but a path was cut into the rocks. It was raining that morning, but I didn't care. I wanted a long, hard walk.

It was nearly noon when I got to the top. I looked down at all the beauty below me. I felt good. Then, suddenly, I saw a form of a man. He was far below me, but was climbing toward me. How quickly he moved! He jumped from rock to rock, like a mountain goat. He seemed to care nothing about falling.

As he got closer, I saw how big the man was. My heart sank. It was the monster! I shook all over with anger and horror. This was my chance to get him. Even if I died trying, I would even the score for poor William and Justine. As soon as he was close enough, I cried out, "You devil! How dare you even come close to me? Come a little closer and I will kill you! I will crush you. You are a monster! If killing you would bring back the people you killed, I would kill you a thousand times!"

The monster did not try to harm me. He just gave me a horrible smile and said, "I thought you'd act this way. People always hate those who are low and unlucky. And I am the unluckiest creature of all. Even the lowest man in the world is loved by his creator. Frankenstein, you are my creator. Yet you hate me! You and I are tied together, forever, until one of us is dead."

He pointed his finger at me. "And you talk of killing me. What kind of man are you? You gave me life—a life of horror. All men are turned against me. I did not choose to be the thing you made me. You owe me something, Frankenstein. If you don't give me what you owe me, I will kill every last friend you have. I will kill the rest of your family. The deaths you have seen so far will be nothing!"

"You devil!" I cried. I jumped at him. He got away from me easily.

"Careful, Frankenstein," the creature said. "I am much stronger and bigger than you are. You made me so. I could break you like a dry twig. But I won't do that. You are my creator, and I cannot raise my hand against you.

"You call me a devil. But I would not have been this way. Life has made me a killer. I would have been like an angel. But after you gave me life, you left me. You turned away from me. I have been evil because I am unhappy. Make me happy, Frankenstein, and I will be the best and kindest creature on earth."

His words made me more angry. "You talk of happiness, when you have caused such pain?" I asked. "Oh, you evil creature! Go away! I can't stand to look at you. I can't stand to listen to you."

"Hear me out, Frankenstein," the monster said. "Even a man on trial gets a chance to tell his story. I don't have anyone who loves me. Everyone's hand is raised against me. And it is not my fault. You must hear me out."

I thought about what the creature was saying. I *was* his creator. Maybe I did owe him some happiness. Maybe I should listen to what he had to say. The creature told me to follow him. He led me to a hut, a few hundred feet below the top of the mountain. It was there that he told me his story.

Chapter 7

"It is hard for me to remember the early days of my life. All I really remember is light and dark. I know now what was happening to me. I was born fully grown. I could see, feel, hear, and smell. But inside, I was a baby—a newborn child.

"When you ran from me, I didn't know why. How could I know what an ugly thing I was? Without knowing why, I took a coat from your house, and left. I went deep into the woods. I slept on the wet ground. I ate what I could find—mostly berries and roots. All during this time, I was sad. But I didn't know why.

"One day, I found what was left of a campfire. I was excited by this wonderful thing. It gave warmth and light. Like a baby who doesn't know better, I tried to touch it. Of course, it burned me. In this way, I learned about fire. Because I had no father or mother to teach me, I had to learn the hard way. All of my early lessons were learned this way.

"I also learned a hard lesson when I met people for the first time. I found a poor hut in the woods. I went to the door and saw an old man inside. He was making his breakfast. When I came near him, he took one look at me and began screaming. He ran away. I didn't know why. You see, I didn't know I was so ugly. And I couldn't even ask why the man ran. I didn't know how to speak.

"The same thing happened when I came upon a small town in the woods. I began to walk down the main street. Right away, people began screaming and running. Men threw sticks and stones at me. They drove me away. I ran into the woods where I was safe. Then I sat down and cried. Why did people treat me this way?

"Before long, the weather began to turn cold. I didn't know how to build a house for myself. Then, deep in the woods, I found a small cottage. Next to the cottage there was a tiny shack. I slept in the shack at night. I hid in the woods during the day.

"I found a small crack in the cottage wall. It was on the side where my shack was. At night, I could hide in the shack and look through the crack at the people inside. Three people lived in the cottage: an old man, a young man, and a young woman.

"I couldn't believe my eyes. These people had a way to make a room bright at night! I had never seen candles or lamps before. And the old man did something that was even more wonderful. He played a guitar and sang. At first, I didn't know what the instrument was. But, oh, the music! It was beautiful!

"The young man and woman sang along. I never knew the sweet sound of singing before. I thought, 'These must be the luckiest people in the world. Look at all the wonderful things they have.' I couldn't understand why their songs were so sad. I thought of what I had—bare ground to sleep on

and no one to love or care for me. Then I was sure that these three people had everything.

"It took me some time to find out that they were very poor. The two young people often gave their food to the old man. Then they wouldn't eat. That is how I learned that there wasn't enough food for all of them.

"Suddenly, I felt very bad. You see, I had been stealing food from their little garden. I thought they had plenty of food. I almost cried to think of what I had done to them. I stopped taking their food. I went back into the woods for acorns and berries.

"I spent most of the winter in the shack. By watching the family, I learned something wonderful. I didn't know what language was. But I heard these people make sounds to each other. Sometimes the sounds made the people smile. Sometimes the sounds made them sad.

"Slowly, I began to learn words. My first words were *fire, milk, bread,* and *wood.* As I learned to speak and listen, I found out about the people in the cottage. They all had names. The girl was called sister or Agatha. The boy was called brother or Felix. They called the old man Father.

"The more I watched these people, the more I began to care about them. When they were unhappy, I felt sad. When they were happy, I also felt happy.

"Then, in the spring, things changed. Another young woman came to live in the cottage. Her name was Safie. Felix greeted her with great warmth. Somehow, he was different with her than he was with his sister Agatha. It took me some time to figure out why. It was the first time I had seen a man and woman in love.

"From listening to Safie talk with Felix and Agatha, I learned a lot about the family. Their last name was DeLacy. They were from France. At one time, they had been rich. Safie's father was a good friend of the family. But Safie's father got into bad trouble with the government. The DeLacys tried to help him, but that got them in trouble, too. They lost everything they had. They had to run away to Germany and live in this small cottage. Then, Safie's father died. She came to live with the DeLacys.

"Safie and Felix were planning to marry. They were very much in love. Safie did not know how to read and write. So Felix was going to teach her. I saw that this was my great chance. When Safie got her lessons in reading and writing, I watched and listened. That is how I learned to read."

Chapter

"Not long after I had learned to read, something happened that really opened my eyes. One day, I was in the woods looking for food. I found a box with three books inside. I was very lucky. The books were written in French—the language I had learned.

"Until that time, all I knew of the world was what I had seen in the cottage. I read the books I found, and I learned what life was like outside the DeLacy family. I learned about human feelings. I learned some history.

"One book told a story about God at war with His heavenly creatures. This was more than a tale to me. Then I came to the part about the creation of Adam. I wondered where my creator was. Had he turned from me, as God had from Satan?

"At this time, I read another book. It was in the pocket of the coat I took from your house, Frankenstein. Now that I could read, I opened it. It was the notebook you wrote in during the four months before you created me. In a short time, I had read this notebook.

"Now I knew who and what I was. And, more important, I knew who my creator was.

"I give these notes back to you, Frankenstein. I now know everything about my birth. I know, too, what an evil person you are. How I hate the day you gave me life!

"You made me ugly and horrible. I have lived a life of sadness. All hands are raised against me. People run when they see me. And I am alone, always alone. Even the lowest animal on earth has a friend. But I don't. I am alone. All I have, Frankenstein, is you. Yet you ran away from me on the very night you gave me life. You must have no heart.

"But there is more to my story. One beautiful autumn day, Agatha, Felix, and Safie went into town. The old man was left alone in the cottage. I had learned much about him and his family. I knew why the young people helped him so much. He was blind.

"Knowing that DeLacy was blind might help me. Up until now, I had never spoken to a living soul. There was no one for me to speak to. Besides, I knew from my early days that people would run from me. DeLacy could not see how ugly I was. I wanted to talk with him. But I was afraid to take this chance. I don't know how long I stood at the cottage door, afraid to knock. I almost ran away a few times. Finally, I knocked on the door.

" 'Who is there?' asked the old man. 'Come in.'

"I stepped inside. 'Pardon me,' I said to DeLacy.

41

'I am a tired traveler in need of rest. May I sit a few minutes by your fire?'

" 'Of course,' the old man said. 'I'm afraid I can't be of much help to you. I can't offer you any food. We have so little.'

"He couldn't know that I had seen how poor they were. I told DeLacy that I had food. I said that all I needed was a little rest by the fire.

"I sat down. For a few minutes we did not talk. I didn't know what to do next. I had never talked with anyone before. Finally, the old man spoke.

" 'You speak my language. Are you French?'

"I smiled as I answered his question. 'No,' I said. 'But I was taught by a French family.' This was quite true. But the old man didn't know that I meant *his* family.

" 'And what brings you to Germany?' he asked.

"It was easy for me to explain why I was there. 'I have come to see the family that taught me,' I said. 'They are wonderful people. In my way, I love them all. But they have never seen me. I am afraid they won't like me. They may chase me away. If they do that, I will have no friends in all the world.'

" 'Don't worry, stranger,' the old man said to me. 'If these people are as good as you say, they would never chase you away. Why should they?'

"I told DeLacy that I was not very pleasant to look at. And that I was afraid that the family

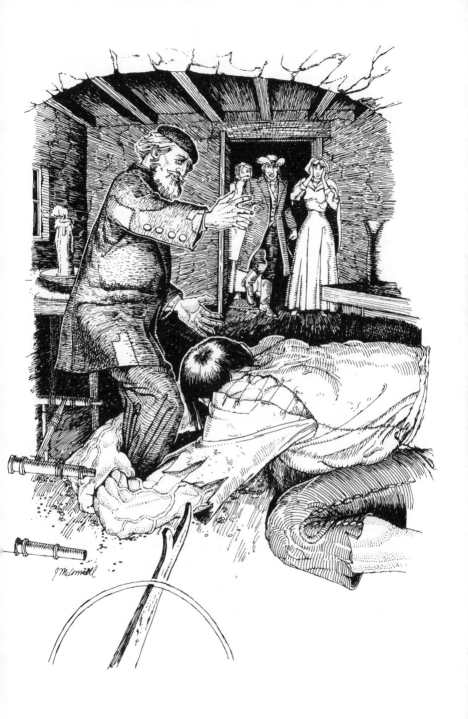

would only see how ugly I was on the outside. They might never know how much I loved them.

" 'As to your looks, I do not know,' said the old man. 'I am blind. But why not trust these people you love so? If you have done nothing wrong, they will not drive you away. If you tell me your story, maybe I can help you. Do these people live near here?'

"I told him that the family lived very close by. Then he asked me the name of the family. Just as I was about to answer, the young people came back to the cottage. My heart was filled with fear. 'Now is the time!' I cried. 'You can save me. The family I spoke of is yours. Don't let Felix, Agatha, and Safie drive me away!'

"DeLacy stood up in surprise. 'Great God!' he yelled. 'Who are you?' I fell to my knees, and wrapped my arms around the old man's legs. 'Save me!' I cried, as the cottage door opened.

"Then the three young people walked in and saw me. Agatha fainted, and Safie ran screaming from the cottage. Felix tore me away from the old man. He picked up a stick and began to hit me. I could have torn him to pieces. But I thought of how much I loved the DeLacys. I also thought about how much I had learned from them. With tears in my eyes, I ran from the cottage."

Chapter **9**

"I spent the night hiding in the woods. Once the sun came up, I began to think more clearly. It had been a mistake to speak to the old man that way. I should have stayed only a minute or so. If I had done this a few times, he would have gotten used to speaking to me. Then things might have turned out differently.

"I went back to the shack and hid in the bushes. I looked for old DeLacy. I didn't see him. Felix was there. He was talking to a man I had never seen before. The stranger seemed angry. 'This will cost you all you have,' he said to Felix.

" 'I don't care,' Felix said. 'We cannot stay here. My father's life is in danger. You don't know. You didn't see the thing that had hold of him.'

"And so, the DeLacys moved away. The only happiness in my life went with them. Once again, I was alone in the world. I heard men out in the woods. I was sure they were looking for the 'terrible thing.' They were looking for me. But where could I go?

"I stopped feeling sad. I began to feel angry. One night, I went back to the cottage. I burned it down.

Then I began to think about you, Frankenstein. It was your fault that my life was so unhappy. I decided to punish you.

"I looked in your notebook. I saw that you lived in Geneva. I remembered from Safie's lessons that Geneva was in Switzerland. I began to walk from Germany to Switzerland. It was a long, hard trip. Crossing mountains the way I did would have killed any other man. I would have welcomed death. But you made me too strong, Frankenstein. The trip didn't kill me.

"I was in Switzerland when another awful thing happened. I was out in the woods when I heard voices. I hid behind a tree, near a fast mountain stream. A little girl ran out of the trees. She was laughing. Far behind her, I heard other voices. The girl must have been playing hide-and-seek.

"She wasn't watching where she was running. She got too close to the stream, and slipped into the fast waters. She screamed. I saw her, and jumped in after her. The waters were strong. Any other man could not have saved her. But I did.

"I got her safely to the side of the stream. As soon as she got a good look at me, she began to scream for help. 'Please, I won't hurt you,' I said. But it was no use. She kept screaming. Just then, a group of men ran out of the woods. One of them had a gun. He fired at me, and I was hit in the shoulder. Before he could shoot again, I ran deeper into the woods.

"I was in terrible pain. I didn't know if the bullet was still in my shoulder or not. It didn't matter. I had no way of getting it out. Still, I kept walking toward Geneva.

"As I walked, I thought, 'So this is what I get for being good: I get shot.' I thought again of who had caused this pain. It wasn't the man with the gun. It was you, Frankenstein. You had made me the ugly thing I am. But I would get back at you, once I got to Geneva.

"After two months, I finally reached Geneva. I found a quiet place near the lake and hid myself. I thought about all that had happened in my short life. As the sun went down, I heard some sounds in the bushes nearby. Suddenly, a little child burst upon my hiding place.

"He was a beautiful child. He had blond hair and blue eyes. I looked at him. He was so young and sweet. I thought, 'Maybe I can talk to this boy. He hasn't lived long enough to think I'm ugly. Children will trust. They haven't been taught to hate yet.'

"Thinking this, I grabbed the boy's hand. As soon as he saw me, he put his hands in front of his eyes and screamed. 'Child, why are you screaming?' I asked. 'I won't hurt you. Just listen to me!'

47

" 'Let me go, you monster!' he cried. 'You want to tear me into pieces, and eat me all up! Let me go, or I'll tell my papa!'

"I held onto his hand. I told him to come with me or he would never see his family again.

" 'No, I won't go with you!' the child cried. 'Let me go, or my papa will take care of you. He's an important man. He's Mr. Frankenstein. Don't you dare hurt me!'

"As soon as I heard the name, I became angry. 'Frankenstein!' I cried. 'You belong to *him*? I promised myself I would get even with Frankenstein. And I will start with you!' The child began to scream even more. I tried to quiet him. I grabbed his throat. But I am so strong, and the child was so small . . . in a moment, he was dead.

"At first, I felt bad. Then I was filled with joy. I even clapped my hands in hellish joy. This child belonged to your family. I would show you. I would bring as much sadness to you as you had to me!

"As I looked down at the child, I saw something on his coat. It was a pin with a picture of a beautiful woman on it. I took it. I walked away, looking at the lovely face. It was a kind face. As I looked at it, I began to feel better. But then I became angry again. Such a woman would never look at me without hatred in her eyes.

"I walked on. Soon I came to a barn. A pretty young woman was sleeping inside. I bent over her and whispered sweet words of love to her. She moved in her sleep. I drew back. I knew that if she woke up, she would see me and scream. A woman could never be my friend.

"Suddenly, I was filled with anger at her. She would run from me if she saw me. She would never know what I was really like inside. She would see me only as an ugly monster. Well, if she would make me suffer, then she would suffer, too.

"From listening to Felix, I had learned something about the law. If the pin was found on her, the police would blame her for the boy's death. I slipped it into her pocket. Then I ran away from the barn.

"I have stayed near Geneva since then. I knew that one day I would find you, Frankenstein. Now I have. You will never be rid of me. I will bring sadness and harm to all you love, unless you do one thing for me.

"I am alone, and everyone runs from me. I want company. I want someone as ugly as I am. Frankenstein, you will create another like me. But this one will be a woman. You will make a wife for me!"

Chapter

When the monster finished his story, I didn't know what to say. At first, I told him that I would not make a wife for him. I was not going to make another monster that would hurt people.

"Don't you see?" the creature answered. "I'm evil only because I am so unhappy. If I have company, I won't be sad. And we will not stay near people. They would hate us and want to hurt us. I will take my wife to another country, far away from any people."

When he made this promise, I told the monster that I would make a wife for him. He said, "Begin your work soon. I will be there when it is time for her to meet me."

I returned home. I spoke to no one about my meeting with the creature. How could I? I knew now that I had to make another monster. If I didn't, the creature would destroy everyone who was close to me.

I began to look over the notebook that the monster had returned to me. I found that I couldn't make another creature without many months of study. But my heart wasn't in it at all. I put off starting the work for weeks.

51

Then I read about some new discoveries in England. They could take months off my work. I had to speak to the scientists in England. I told my father that I wanted to go to England for a while. Of course, I didn't tell him why.

To my surprise, my father thought the trip was a great idea. He had been worried about how quiet and sad I had been. He felt that travel would do me good. He thought that my friend Henry should go along with me. I knew that I couldn't let Henry know what I was planning to do. But I also couldn't say that I didn't want my best friend to travel with me.

Once in England, I went to Oxford University. I spoke with the best scientists. I took notes. The scientists in England saved me months, maybe years, of work. But I needed a secret place to work.

Henry and I decided to take a vacation. We traveled north. The countryside was beautiful. We saw wonderful places, but something kept bothering me. I knew that my vacation would be over soon. I knew that I would have to find a place where I could work in secret. Then I would have to begin making a woman for the monster. I would again have to rob graves and cut up bodies. It was hard to enjoy my trip when I thought about these things.

I also had the feeling that I was being watched. When looking out on a beautiful lake or field, I would catch something out of the corner of my eye. Was it a person? Or was it the monster following me? I couldn't shake off this feeling.

Finally, I found the place I was looking for. It was an island near Scotland. Hardly anyone lived there anymore. But there were three huts that I could use. They were perfect for me. I began my work.

Henry did not live on the island with me. He decided to travel to Scotland and Ireland. We agreed to meet in a few months. I knew that Henry must not find out what terrible things I was doing on the island.

When I made the first creature, I didn't know how it would turn out. I had high hopes to keep me going. I had dreamed that I was creating life. My plan was to make the world a better place. I dreamed that maybe I could even give life back to the dead.

But I had no such dreams when making the second creature. Instead, I had fears. What if she turned out to be as ugly and horrible as the first creature? I had learned from the monster. Because he was ugly, the world had turned against him— had made him a killer. Would the same thing happen to a woman I created?

But I had other fears, too. My new creature might be very different from the first one. She might not want to be kind. She might choose to be evil. The monster had promised that he would take his wife away from people. Maybe she would not agree to go! And there was no way to know how she would feel about the monster. She might hate him as everyone else did. Then there would be *two* angry monsters loose in the world!

But what if the creatures did go away together? What if they had children? What terrible things would their children be? I would have created an entire race of monsters!

One day, I looked down at the large body on the table. The woman was almost finished. I looked up. There, at the window, was the monster! He *had* followed me. He was watching me as I worked. He had a horrible smile on his face. He was waiting for his wife.

Suddenly, the whole thing made me sick. I couldn't go through with my plans. I couldn't let two of these things loose upon the world. With a wild cry, I tore apart everything on the table. My work was destroyed. The monster saw what I did. He let out a cry of anger. Then he ran off.

I left the workshop and went to my bedroom. I sat there for hours. Suddenly, I heard a sound. I looked up. The monster stood before me.

"Go away!" I cried. "I won't do it. I can't do what you want!"

"You dare break your promise to me?" the monster asked. "I have followed you all the way from Switzerland. I have lived like an animal, just to be near you. I wanted to be there when my wife first opened her eyes. Now you have destroyed her!"

"Yes, I have," I replied. "And I can't keep my promise. I will not turn another monster like you loose upon the world."

"I tried reasoning with you, Frankenstein," the monster said. "But hear me now. Remember, I have power. You think you're unhappy now? You have no idea what I can do. I will make you curse the day you were born!"

I told the creature that he could not change my mind. "Go away, you evil creature," I yelled. "I can't stand to look at you!"

The monster stared at me. I thought for a minute that he would attack me. Then he got hold of himself. "Very well, Frankenstein," he said. "I will go. But you have not seen the last of me. I will be with you on your wedding night!"

Then he was gone. I returned to my workshop. I gathered up all the dead body parts, and put them into a sack. I took my small boat out to sea. I rowed for hours. Then I threw the terrible things into the water. Feeling tired, I sat back to rest for a few minutes. I must have fallen asleep.

When I woke up, a storm had come up. I couldn't see land. I had no way of knowing where I was. I don't know how I did it, but I kept the boat from going under. When the sun came up the next morning, I saw land.

I made it to shore. As soon as I landed, a man came up to me, "You will come with me, right away," he said. "I am taking you to a judge, and then to jail."

"What's this all about?" I asked. "I don't know where I am. I never knew that Englishmen were so rude."

"I don't know about Englishmen," the man said. "This is Ireland. And we aren't kind to murderers."

My mind was spinning. What could this be about? "I have done no wrong," I told the man. "I was lost in a storm off Scotland all night."

"You can tell that to the judge," the man said.

Chapter 11

I was taken to the judge's office. Three men there told the judge what they had seen. They were out fishing the night of the storm. They found they couldn't make it back to town. They had to tie up their boat about two miles up the coast.

There, they found the body of a man. He was a good-looking man who was about twenty-five years old. At first, they thought he had drowned. But his clothes weren't wet. They took him to a nearby cottage. In the light, they saw that he had been murdered. The marks of the murderer's fingers were still on his neck.

The first part of their story didn't interest me. But then I heard the part about finger marks on the neck. I thought about poor William.

Then the man talked about how I came to be in their town. They said that I couldn't have come from Scotland in such a storm. I must have been in this town all along. They believed that the storm had stopped me from getting away. They thought I had killed the young man they found!

The judge listened to all this without saying a word. Then he said, "Let us show the body to this stranger."

I went along, gladly. I knew I had done no wrong. I guess they thought that a murderer would tell the truth when faced with the crime. I followed them into a room next to the judge's office. Then I saw the body. It was Henry! The monster had killed my best friend! The room around me went black as I passed out and fell to the floor.

I can't remember much about the next three months. I knew that there were kind hands that cared for me. I saw faces above my bed. Some were angry; others were kind.

I saw that I was in a jail cell. After a while, I began to come back to the real world again. Think of my joy when one day my father came to visit me. It didn't take long for him to set things right. A trial was held, and I was found not guilty.

Because I was still sick, my father took me to Paris. Doctors there could help me. We stayed in Paris for a long time. Then, one day, I got a letter from Elizabeth.

She thought I didn't love her anymore. She still loved me. But she told me in her letter that if I no longer wanted to get married, it was all right. How could I tell her of my love? The only reason we were not married was that the monster had said, "I shall be with you on your wedding night."

But it had been some time since I had seen the monster. Maybe he was dead. Surely, any man with a gun who saw the ugly creature would try to kill him. I wrote to Elizabeth. I told her that we would be married soon. My father and I returned to Geneva. We began to get ready for the wedding.

All the time we were planning the wedding, I kept thinking of what the monster had said. I bought a few guns and knives. The monster might be dead. But if he were alive, I would be ready for him. I was not going to die on my wedding night!

We had a wonderful wedding. I was very happy. All that had happened began to fade from my mind. We set off on our honeymoon. We reached our hotel at eight o'clock that night. A thunderstorm came up.

There was no sign of the monster. But I didn't want to take any chances. I took a gun and a candle. I set out to check each room in the hotel. Elizabeth was getting ready for bed.

I was in the basement when I heard Elizabeth scream. Suddenly, I knew that the monster wasn't planning to kill me. He was after Elizabeth. I ran upstairs and into our bedroom. Elizabeth was lying across the bed, dead. Finger marks were on her neck.

I looked up just then. Lightning flashed at the window. And there, looking in, was the monster! The evil creature was smiling. I aimed my gun at him and fired. I missed. He ran off, and was lost in the storm. Men from the hotel helped me look for the monster, but we couldn't find him. It was as if the earth itself hid the evil creature.

I felt a sadness I had never known before. I had never felt so lonely. I returned to Geneva as soon as I could. When I told my father what had happened, it was too much for him. I think he had loved Elizabeth more than any of the Franken-stein family. A few days later, he died of a broken heart.

As I stood at my father's grave, my thoughts went racing back. The monster had kept his prom-ise. William, Justine, Henry, Elizabeth, and now my father were dead because of him. A darkness covered my eyes, and I fell to the ground.

I spent the next two months in a madhouse. My mind was gone. When I came back to my right mind, there was more trouble. I had to go before a judge to tell about Elizabeth's murder. I decided to tell the judge the full story. I knew that I was taking a chance. Anyone hearing the tale would be sure I was out of my mind. Yet, I had to tell the truth. I showed the judge that I couldn't be mad—how all the parts of the story fit together too well for that. Thank God, he believed me.

"But what can I do about it?" asked the judge. "I would help you if I could. But this creature could be anywhere. He followed you across Europe. The weather does not seem to bother him. And he is stronger than any man."

"It doesn't matter," I told the judge. "I will go after him alone. He is never far from me. He stays near me to enjoy all the sadness he has brought to my life. He laughs at what he has done. I will find the evil creature, and I will kill him. Or I will spend the rest of my life trying!"

61

Chapter 12

I decided to leave Geneva forever. Too much had happened there. But, before I left, I visited the graves of William, Elizabeth, and my father. I stood there, looking down at the gravestones. Suddenly, I heard a laugh from the darkness. It was the monster! "I am happy now, Frankenstein," the voice said. "You will be unhappy for the rest of your life. You will be alone—just as I am." Then it laughed again.

I ran to the spot where the voice had come from. There was no one there. Just then, the moon broke through the clouds. I could see the monster, running so fast that no man could catch him. I tried to follow him, but he left me far behind.

Since that night, I have chased the monster all over the world. He has never gone near towns and cities. He knows that people would see him and try to kill him. But now and then, someone spots him, and tells me. In this way, I have been able to follow him.

Every time I want to give up, I think of William, Justine, Elizabeth, Henry, and my father. Often when I think I've lost him, the monster leaves messages for me. He cuts them into trees or on rocks. I know he does this to give me more pain. It works. But it also makes me chase him harder.

Once I saw him get on a boat going to the Black Sea. I took the boat, too. I looked in every part of the boat. But I couldn't find him. Later, I picked up his trail again.

I grew thin. My only food was the wild animals I could kill. As I got farther north, I found one last note from the monster. It said: *Get ready! The worst is still ahead of you. Get warm clothes and plenty of food. We are going to a cold, icy place. I will laugh as you suffer.*

I bought a sled and some dogs to pull it. I bought food. The monster was so far north that he was almost at the ocean. I found a small village. The people had seen the creature. They told me of a giant who came to their village. He had guns and knives. He drove away a poor family. He stole their winter food supply, sled, and dogs. He headed north.

I went after him. I stopped only to rest and feed my dogs. I would not sleep at peace until I caught him. Sometimes, he was only a day ahead of me. Once, I saw him. He was far, far away on the ice. I went after him.

Just as I was getting close, the ice broke up. Cold blue water was between me and the monster. Before long, he was gone. I haven't seen him since. I floated on a broken piece of ice for many weeks.

All but one of my dogs died. I was close to death myself. Then your ship found me.

You probably wondered why I asked you where your ship was going. As I have said, I will never give up my search for the creature. If you had been going back to England, I would not have gone with you. You are headed north—where I am sure the creature has gone. That is why I am happy to have come on board.

And that is my story. I have lost the monster. I would ask you to help me find him. But it wouldn't be fair. You want to go on to the North Pole. It is the dream of your life. I just ask this: If I die, and you find the monster, show him no mercy. He may talk sweetly. He may tell you how everyone has treated him badly. But he is the king of liars.

His words may begin to change your mind. But remember William, Justine, Henry, Elizabeth, and my father. They all died because of him. Don't stop to think. Kill him! Only then will my soul rest in peace.

Ending Letters

To: Mrs. Saville, England
September 5, 17_ _

Dear Sister,

You have read this strange story. Does it make your blood run as cold as it does mine? Sometimes I thought Frankenstein was not strong enough to finish it. His voice often broke. Tears would come to his eyes.

The question is: Do I believe the story? Frankenstein showed me letters written by Felix and Safie, the young couple in the cottage. The way he told the story makes it seem real. Yes, I believe the monster lives.

Frankenstein saw that I was taking notes while he told his story. He asked to see them. When I showed them to him, he made some changes. He wanted to make sure I told the story correctly. Then I asked how he gave life to the monster. He said, "Have you gone mad? Didn't you learn from my tale? Never again will such a creature be made. I will take the secret with me to my grave!"

I am sure that Frankenstein is a little mad—but only when he speaks of the monster. When we talk of other things, he is great company. Oh, the things he knows, and the things he has read! I wrote before of finding a friend. I wanted someone to talk with. I have found him in Victor Frankenstein. I told him so.

"Poor Walton," he said to me. "I would love to be your friend. But I cannot. Think back on my friend Henry. Look at what happened to him and all those around me, all those whom I loved. I cannot have friends. Because the monster lives alone, I must also live alone. He has seen to that.

"There is only one thing more I must do in my life," Frankenstein continued. "I must hunt and kill the monster. After that, I can die in peace. I cannot make new friends. I cannot love again. I must destroy the monster. Then I will be ready for the darkness of the grave."

September 8

My Dear Sister,

I fear we are lost. The ice has closed around us again. Everywhere we look we see mountains of white ice. The men have been acting badly. They want a promise from me. If we can get out of this ice, they want me to sail back for home. I must give up my dream.

A few months ago, I would not have agreed to do this. But I have learned from Frankenstein's story.

He, too, had a dream. He followed that dream, and see what it cost him! If I follow my dream, it may cost the lives of all the men on this ship. I cannot do this, so I have given my promise to them.

Meanwhile, Frankenstein's health is failing. He grows sicker and thinner each day. He seems alive only when he talks of his hunt for the monster. His eyes shine, and he tries to get out of bed. But he is too weak. He doesn't seem to care if he lives or dies.

The ice is all around us. I don't know if this letter will ever reach you. I send you all my love . . . and the memory of a broken dream.

September 12

The ice has broken! The men are happy. They know I will keep my promise. They know they are going home. I know we must go back. But I am unhappy that I must forget about my dream.

I went down to Frankenstein's cabin to tell him the news. He sat up in his bed. "Then you are turning back?" he asked.

"Yes, I must," I replied. "I have given the men my promise."

"Good," Frankenstein said. "Go in peace. Return to England. Live your life without dreams that you should not have. It is good to have a dream. But when that dream harms others, it becomes evil. I

had hoped to create life. But some things are best left to nature.

Frankenstein shook my hand. "I wish you well, Walton," he said. "God keep you safe on your trip home. But I cannot go with you. I must find and destroy the monster. I am still weak, but heaven will give me strength. The creature cannot be allowed to live."

With this, Frankenstein tried to get out of bed. He was too weak. He fell back, and passed out. I thought for a moment that he had died. But in a few minutes, his eyes opened again.

"I'm afraid I'm dying," he said. "And it hurts to know that the monster still lives. I have gone over my life in my mind. I think I did no wrong. My reason for creating the monster was a good one: I wanted to help humankind. Yes, it is true that I ran out on the creature I made. But I couldn't help it, once I saw how it looked.

"And I think I was right when I would not make a wife for him. He had shown what he was like. He had killed William and had caused Justine's death. I couldn't know for sure that he wouldn't kill again. And if there were a whole race of these creatures, who would be safe?

"I wish I could ask you to take up my hunt for the monster. I can't do that. You have your own life to live. But if you should ever come across the evil *creature, kill it! Don't stop for a second. And now . . ."*

His voice faded away. He lay back on the bed. I took his hand. He weakly pressed my hands. Then his body gave a small shake, and he was still. For the first time since I met him, I saw a peaceful smile upon his face. Victor Frankenstein had died.

I must stop writing now. Something is going on below decks. I hear a sound like a human voice. But somehow it is different. I have to go see what is happening. I will finish this letter when I come back to my cabin . . .

Great God, what I have just seen! I must write it down. My mind is spinning. I feel as if I may go mad—madder than poor Victor Frankenstein.

The sounds I heard were coming from Frankenstein's cabin. I went in. A big shape was standing over Frankenstein's body. I would be lying if I said it was a man. The awful sounds I heard were coming from this thing.

Its long hair was black, shiny, and ragged. The hair covered its face. One hand was reaching out, as if to touch Frankenstein. I saw the hand. It was yellow and wrinkled, like a mummy's. It was Frankenstein's monster!

It heard me come in. It turned to face me. Never in my life have I seen such a face. I cannot find the

words to tell how ugly and horrible it was. I had to turn away.

I was afraid that the monster would leave. "Stay," I said. The monster looked at me in surprise. Then it looked back at the dead body of its creator. It went back to Frankenstein's bedside, as if I weren't there at all.

"I have killed him, too!" cried the monster. "With him, it is ended." The creature leaned over the dead body and said, "Frankenstein, I am sorry. I am sorry for all the misery I caused you. But you can't hear me now." The creature gave a cry of sadness.

I looked at the monster. I almost felt sorry for it. Then I remembered what Frankenstein had told me. I thought of all the lives this creature had taken. I was afraid of the monster, yet I had to speak.

"Being sorry won't help," I said. "It's too late. You should have thought of that before you began killing. If you'd had any good in you, Frankenstein would still be alive."

"Do you think I wanted to be evil?" the monster asked. "Do you think the cries of poor Henry were music to my ears? I am a gentle creature. My heart was made to receive love—not to be filled with hate! When Frankenstein destroyed my wife, I went mad with sadness. I wanted to give Frankenstein a taste of the unhappiness he had given me. That is why I had to kill Henry. I couldn't stop myself.

"Once I came to my senses, I hated myself for what I had done. I went back to Switzerland. I was going to live in the woods. I would see no one. I would be kind and gentle to all who crossed my path.

"Then I heard of Frankenstein's plan to marry. How dare he be happy, when I was so alone? The madness came over me again. I couldn't stop myself. Do you know the pain it caused me to kill Elizabeth? I can still hear her cries. But I was like Satan cast out of Paradise. Evil had become my God.

"I enjoyed leading Frankenstein across the world. I enjoyed leaving notes to drive him on. I laughed as he went through the ice and cold, which didn't bother me.

"But now, he is dead. It is over. I have returned to my right mind. You can't know how sorry I am. If only I could tell my creator how sorry I am. But it's too late!"

I looked at the ugly creature before me. I remembered that Frankenstein had told me that this monster was the king of liars. "Liar!" I said. "You're only sorry because it's over. You cannot hurt Frankenstein anymore. He is at peace. You can't get to him. That's all you're sorry about!"

"I know why you think that," the monster said. "But all you heard was Frankenstein's story. Yes, I destroyed his dreams and his life. But it didn't make me feel any better. It made me feel worse. I didn't ask him to create me. He made me so ugly that no man could look upon me. Did I ask for that?

"I always hoped that someone, somewhere, would see beyond my outside looks. I dreamed that I would find someone who would know my gentle heart. I wanted someone to love me. My creator did not. I asked only that he make a wife for me. I would have gone away with her. We would have lived in the jungles, where no one would see us. I would have had someone to love—someone to love me.

"But I was never to have a wife. Frankenstein saw to that. Yet, he called me a monster. Who is the real monster? What about the farmer? I saved his child from drowning. But he shot me. Is he not a monster for doing that? Frankenstein made me what I am. Then he ran from me. He gave me a life without love or friends. Is he not a monster for doing that? The life I had to live drove me mad. In my madness, I killed.

"Even now, I cry for Frankenstein. You see, I am not just a creature of evil. I am what Frankenstein and the world have made me."

I looked at the creature. I wondered if I should do what Frankenstein had asked. Should I kill this thing before it could do any more harm to the world? But I had no gun and no knife or sword. The monster was strong. It could break me in half. It seemed as if the creature read my thoughts.

"Don't worry," it said to me. "I am finished with evil. It is over now. No other person will die at my hands. It is now time for me to die. And I will take care of that quickly.

"I came to the ship on a floating piece of ice. It is still by the side of your ship. I will float away to the land of ice and snow. Without food, even I shall die. I shall die as I lived: alone, without love, and hated by all."

The creature looked down at the body of Frankenstein. "Good-bye, my creator," it said. "I made a hell of your life. But it was nothing like the hell I had to live through."

Saying this, the monster jumped through the open window of the cabin. It landed below on the piece of ice. It was soon carried away by the waves and lost in the darkness.